SoRting out WORRY

DEDICATION

Lyn — for your continuing support over a long journey.
A wonderful companion.

SORTING OUT WORRY

GRANT BRECHT

PRENTICE HALL

Sydney   New York   Toronto   Mexico   New Delhi
London   Tokyo   Singapore   Rio de Janeiro

Acquisitions Editor: Kaylie Smith
Production Editor: Elizabeth Thomas
Copy Editor: Loretta Barnard
Cover design: Eilish Bouchier
Ilustrations: David Egan

Typeset by DOCUPRO, Lane Cove, NSW

Printed in Australia by Australian Print Group,
  Maryborough, Victoria

1 2 3 4 5 00 99 98 97 96

ISBN 0 7248 1109 5

National Library of Australia
Cataloguing-in-Publication Data

Brecht, Grant Phillip
  Sorting out worry

  Bibliography
  Includes index
  ISBN 0 7248 1109 5

  1. Anxiety. 2. Stress management. I. Title.
  (Series: Sorting out life series).

152.46

Prentice Hall of Australia Pty Ltd, *Sydney*
Prentice Hall, Inc., *Englewood Cliffs, New Jersey*
Prentice Hall Canada, Inc., *Toronto*
Prentice Hall Hispanoamericana, SA, *Mexico*
Prentice Hall of India Private Ltd, *New Delhi*
Prentice Hall International, Inc., *London*
Prentice Hall of Japan, Inc., *Tokyo*
Prentice Hall of Southeast Asia Pty Ltd, *Singapore*
Editora Prentice Hall do Brasil Ltda, *Rio de Janeiro*

PRENTICE HALL

A Division of Simon & Schuster

CONTENTS

PREFACE

Worry is a universal phenomenon, which clearly testifies that as human beings we really do not have 'our act' together. Where are the large black dogs with rabies or those catastrophic happenings or events that a rational person needs to be concerned about? Certainly not in our backyards that often! So what do we worry about and what is the point of our worry?

Well surprise, surprise. Most of our worry, concern and anxiety centres around the 'what if . . .' syndrome. 'What if it doesn't go well . . . what if he/she leaves me . . . what if I get sick . . . what if I lose my job'. So we tend to get tense, preoccupied and moody regarding possible events in our life which generally do not happen. Even if they do, in the greater scheme of things they are hardly catastrophes or major life events and, with proper planning, are usually quite easy to resolve.

Short-term worry which leads us to make adaptive action plans can be very useful. However, that nebulas and ongoing anxiety, fear and concern as we travel through life can have major psychological consequences for us. We can develop anxiety, panic and phobic disorders, become depressed, procrastinate about decisions we need to make and lower the ability of our immune system to fight disease in our bodies.

The most important consequence is that being a chronic worrier detracts us from focusing or enhancing our lives by developing positive, adaptive, rational and solution-oriented attitudes and actions. When we are positive and solution-oriented in life, we quickly *generate options* to deal with whatever is of concern to us. We therefore do away with the need to worry unduly about how terrible and awful that particular happening may be.

This book offers practical and useful techniques to assist you in sorting out adaptive from non-adaptive worry, how it may affect you and what to do about it. You will discover how to control your worry habit and how to recognise when you are successful. Some important tips on living with a worrier are also included.

Enjoy the book and look forward to the future with far less worry and a more positive focus on those invigorating challenges ahead.

Grant Brecht

ACKNOWLEDGMENTS

My sincere gratitude to all who have been encouraging and of assistance in the endeavour to produce this series of books. My appreciation to the many psychologists from whom I have drawn both knowledge and inspiration. Thank you to Kaylie Smith from Prentice Hall for your guidance and enthusiasm for the overall project. Special thanks to Dr John Lang for his assistance in my final realisation that with a desire, focus and "stick-ability", anything in life is truly possible.

Thanks to Lyn and Oliver for ongoing support and tolerance of my efforts to accomplish a goal. Will I ever forget the words of one gorgeous five year old boy 'You're not working on those books again are you Daddy?'

ABOUT THE AUTHOR

Grant Brecht is a Clinical Psychologist who works and lives in Sydney, Australia. He is a sought-after presenter and speaker who is well known for his radio and television appearances assisting people to sort out their lives.

Grant is the Director of CORPsych—a psychological consultancy providing coun- selling and training services to companies and individuals across Australia and New Zealand. He has a unique ability to impart information and assist people to learn psy- chological self-help techniques in a very practical and enjoyable manner.

Look for other books by Grant Brecht in the *Sorting Out* series.

ABOUT THE SERIES

A wise person once remarked that 'Life is not about having no problems, but rather about being able to resolve them quickly when they occur'.

The *Sorting Out* series of books has been written to assist each of us to do just that—to sort out those everyday life challenges that confront everyone of us. Whether it be ongoing and unnecessary worry and anxiety, an inability to plan and set goals in life, low self-esteem and a poor self-image, or too many perceived demands with too few coping strategies, the books in this series will be of immense practical value and benefit.

Our modern lifestyles are demanding and the rapid rate of social and technological change is placing unprecedented pressures on all of us. Quality of life is determine by how well we predict and rise to the challenges which are placed before us on our journey through life. Our ability to communicate effectively is paramount. Effective communication is about remaining flexible, adaptable, rational, positive and solution-orientated, no matter what is happening in our lives.

This very practical and relevant series of books will assist everyone in developing awareness of the issues and topics covered: how we know if it is a problem for us, including the signs and symptoms, and what we can do about it; how we know when we are successful and where to seek further assistance if we need to; and how to live with someone with a particular concern or problem.

The techniques and self-help procedures in the series are drawn from the latest research into the most effective approaches for dealing with the problems and hassles of everyday living.

✖

CHAPTER 1

What is worry?

Life is not about happenings,
But what we say to ourselves about those happenings

Epictetus A.D. c.50–c.138

What if I'm not a good mother?
What if I don't get the job?
What if no one ever loves me again?
What if that lump is cancer?
What if I lose my job?
What if it's not what I really want?

Know the feeling? Don't worry, you're not alone!

Worrying is a very natural human reaction and everybody gets worried or concerned from time to time. Feeling a bit tense, jumpy or irritable is generally a result of worry. When we feel that life is just not worthwhile and that we really are at the 'end of our tether', this too is likely to be due to worry. So what is worry?

DEFINITION OF WORRY

Worry is a human condition consisting of thoughts, actions and emotional responses to certain types of events which may, or we feel may, happen in our lives.

We really can worry about anything if we allow ourselves. Big and small issues, important and unimportant, real or

imaginary, things which are happening or things we feel might happen. The 'what if . . . ?' syndrome is the classic, of course: 'what if it happens . . . ? what if I don't make the team . . .? 'what if I'm not successful?'

We generally experience worry as a feeling or emotional state. We become edgy, jumpy and feel anxious. We may also experience worry more as a thinking and attitudinal state consisting of concerned or negative self-talk. Self-talk is that internal dialogue or conversation in our heads which leads us to react to situations in a particular manner.

Worry may also be experienced as a physical reaction to things in life, real or perceived. We may tense up, frown, begin to talk, walk or eat faster, or maybe slower. So worry is really just one way that human beings can react to any event or events in their lives. Worry may cause a number of, or all of, the following reactions. We may find we are:

◆ apprehensive and edgy;

◆ hesitant;

◆ tense;

2

◆ shaking;

◆ thinking negatively (being pessimistic);

◆ frowning;

◆ emotional;

◆ snappy;

◆ talkative;

◆ passive and withdrawn.

Worrying for short periods of time is generally okay. However, if we find that we develop a worry habit, it can interfere with our quality of life and our ability to enjoy ourselves. Then like any habit, it tends to persist and we may have trouble ridding ourselves of it. It becomes a natural way for us to react, almost as though we are on automatic pilot cruising along with no control. When we feel we cannot control something we start to feel helpless and hopeless in the situation and we may begin to worry even more.

Worry is primarily a thinking state and reaction. Even though we seem to almost automatically feel worried, worry is usually generated by the types of things we are saying to ourselves about what is happening in our lives. The worrying thoughts then lead to emotions or feelings within us, such as feeling anxious, nervous, scared, irritable, sad or depressed, as well as certain actions like shaking, crying, frowning, and withdrawal.

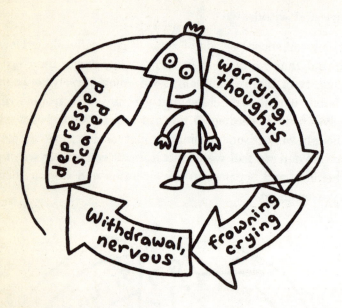

IS WORRYING USEFUL?

Of course some worry can be useful. It may, for example, lead us to avoid dangerous or even injurious situations.

We may spend a little more time thinking about things and so make better decisions for ourselves in the long run. Worry or concern for ourselves means that we may also focus on obtaining and achieving the things we value. We may then also help others, especially those we are close to, to do the same thing. If we are not at all worried or concerned about achieving things in life and having our own needs met, we may go through life pleasing others and neglecting ourselves.

4

So short-term worry and concern which leads to some degree of heightened emotion, which in turn is used to institute effective decision-making and problem-solving is extremely useful and productive.

CASE STUDY

John, 32, was a healthy sporty type who loved the outdoors. His wife, Sue, had been worried about a small dark brown blemish on his back for some months. John dismissed her concerns, feeling she was getting paranoid about a simple freckle. Finally, when the blemish began to blister, Sue insisted John see their doctor who diagnosed a melanoma. Thankfully it was only just below the surface and, after surgery, John was given a clean bill of health. Sue's worry was useful, resulting in appropriate timely action and possibly in saving John's life.

As this example shows, some worry some of the time can be useful. It can help direct and motivate us into useful action. It may assist us in searching for new ways to do things, and so broaden our horizons and help us to mature and grow.

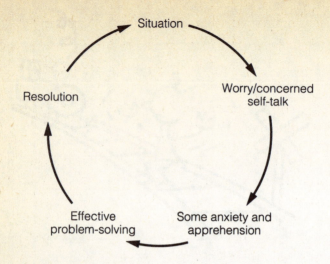

More often than not however, worrying only wastes life. It stops us enjoying activities, planning ahead, taking calculated risks, and interferes with a sense of freedom and control over our own destinies. We can develop a habit of useless, repetitive concerns which run around and around in our heads. Anxiety builds and we start to catastrophise about how terrible things are — that syndrome of making mountains out of molehills. If we do not take appropriate action we can allow the generalised anxiety within us build to the point where we can develop a

phobic disorder or panic disorder. This is the psychologically destructive aspect of non-directed worry.

CASE STUDY

Lorraine, 28, was again on her own after a stormy two and a half year marriage. When she and her husband decided to part, unkind words were exchanged. Lorraine's husband was now living with another woman and seemed very happy. Lorraine worried that she would never find anyone to love her again and that she would be unable to rebuild her life. Her self-confidence suffered, she withdrew from social situations and began to feel extremely lonely and depressed. She felt her life was out of her control and that she would never find happiness again.

When we have a go and try new, exciting and different things, we are more likely to feel confident, self-assured and full of vitality and energy. Worrying will get in the way of all of this if we allow it to. We need to work on ensuring that we do not develop the worry habit, or that we unfreeze the habit if it is with us, and refreeze more adaptive ways of thinking about and reacting to events in our lives.

SUMMARY

◆ Worrying is a natural human response.
◆ Worrying involves thoughts, actions and emotions.
◆ We can worry about anything.
◆ Worry can become a habit.
◆ We can worry automatically.
◆ Thinking patterns play a major part.
◆ Worry can be useful.
◆ Life can be wasted by worry.
◆ We need to develop adaptive thinking and reactions.

CHAPTER 2

Do you worry too much?

WHAT DO WE WORRY ABOUT?

A far shorter answer could be given to 'What don't we worry about?' We can literally worry about anything, and given half a chance, we do. When we begin to focus on what we get anxious and concerned about, some very interesting observations are made. We often actually worry about pleasant events in our lives. This doesn't seem to make sense, does it? Why would we get tense about things in our life that we are looking forward to? Perhaps we like and enjoy worrying so much that we actually go out of our way to find things to get concerned about, even picking on the positive things in our lives! Let's consider what we do tend to worry about to assist us in gaining more awareness about this whole phenomenon.

COMMON THINGS WE WORRY ABOUT

1. *Happiness* — am I happy? am I really contented? could I be doing better? will I still be happy tomorrow? would I be happier somewhere else or with someone else?
2. *Health* — what does that ache mean? will I age well? was the doctor right — am I drinking or smoking too much?
3. *Future* — what will happen to the world? what sort of future will my children have? will I keep up with things? will I have enough money?
4. *Work* — do I really want to do this job? is my career on track? will I get retrenched? am I as smart as I think I am?
5. *Money* — I don't have as much as the Joneses! will interest rates go up? can I afford the mortgage? are we really getting anywhere?
6. *Relationships* — am I happy or could I be happier? am I being taken advantage of? will he or she leave me? will I ever find anybody else? what if they don't like me? am I as good as them?
7. *Marriage* — this is one of those positive events in our life that we can really start to become dramatic about if we allow ourselves: what dress will I wear? who will be my best man? do we invite the people from work? church or a registry? will it last? do I really want this?
8. *Worry* — and of course we can worry about worrying.

This list is actually only the tip of the iceberg in terms of what we can worry about. In fact we can and do worry about anything. Whenever we have nothing to worry about we'll worry about that — the fact we have nothing to worry about. We certainly need to be able to distinguish quickly and effectively between a 'real problem' such as a financial or marital concern, and silly ruminations with no basis in reality. For example, some people

have obsessive thoughts that they may hurt their children, when in fact they have always treated them very well. These types of obsessive worries may need professional help.

What do you worry about? What are the things in life that you find yourself getting upset or concerned about? Use the following exercise to jot some of these down as they come to mind. See if there is a common heading or headings you could place them under, then rate how often and how intense the worry is:

Very frequent	3	I get very worried/upset	3
Frequent	2	I get quite worried	2
Sometimes	1	I get somewhat worried	1
Not at all	0	A little worried for a short time	0

I worry about	How often	Degree of worry
Happiness		
future		
Relationships		

Use this checklist for later reference.

DO YOU WORRY TOO MUCH?

How do we know if we worry too much? How much worry is good for us? When does it start to interfere with our quality of life?

No doubt most of us feel we would like to stop worrying altogether and just take life as it comes, but as we saw in Chapter 1, some worry and concern can be very productive. The trick is to make sure we do not overdo it and only use worry when appropriate, for very short periods of time. We quickly need to be able to move on from an initial worried state to thinking about an action plan to resolve those particular issues we are concerned about.

So do you worry too much? Complete the following checklists to find out.

WORRY CHECKLIST

THINKING/ATTITUDES

Score each question	
Seldom/not much	0
Often/a fair bit	1
Almost all of the time	2

SORTING OUT WORRY

	Score
I think the worst will happen	_____
I often think 'what if something bad happens?'	_____
I think about what I've done wrong	_____
My focus is on what I can't do	_____
The future seems bleak	_____
I worry about other people/my children	_____
I think about bad things in the past	_____
I say 'I can't stand it, it's awful' to myself about things	_____
I am concerned about what others think of me	_____
People will take advantage of me if I'm not careful and alert	_____

Now score each question	
Seldom/not much	2
Often/a fair bit	1
Almost all of the time	0

	Score
I think about how great life is	_____
I think new, unusual things are great	_____
I often think 'now how can I do it?'	_____
I see events as challenges not problems	_____
I look forward to the future	_____
People are generally pleasant and nice	_____
I believe 'if it's to be, it's up to me'	_____
Of course I can make a difference	_____
I am a good person	_____
I believe I give things my best shot	_____
Total score (out of 40)	_____

If you score:

0-10 Your worry is very much in control. It is a psychological and life strength for you, so keep it going.

11-20 Don't panic. At times worrying attitudes are a problem for you. The techniques in the chapters to come will help you to rectify this.

21-30 You probably guessed it — you're a worrier, and have developed the worry habit. Reading this book will help. Persevere with the techniques and reverse the habit.

31-40 Read the book three times and practise, practise, practise — you owe it to yourself. Worry is a real challenge for you, but you can beat it, read on.

BEHAVIOUR/ACTIONS

Score each question	
Seldom/not much	0
Often/a fair bit	1
Almost all the time	2

I don't do things I really want to _____

Many everyday activities in life are dangerous _____

I get quite tense _____

I find myself shaking _____

I jump at loud noises _____

I find myself frowning a lot _____

I have difficulty keeping eye contact with others _____

I don't like meeting new people _____

Concentration is a problem for me _____

I can't stand things to be unfinished _____

SORTING OUT WORRY

Now score each question	
Seldom/not much	2
Often/a fair bit	1
Almost all the time	0

I am relaxed around most people _____

I can generally relax very easily _____

I sleep peacefully for 6-8 hours at night _____

I look forward to new experiences in life _____

I do the things I like doing in life _____

I laugh a lot and see the funny side of life _____

I am friendly and understanding with others _____

I have a good balance of activities in my life _____

I achieve what I set out to do _____

The things I do in life, work/personal, I find rewarding _____

Total score (out of 40) _____

If you scored:

0-10 Well done. Your behaviour, the way you go about your life is indicating little worry, so keep it going.

11-20 There are some indications that your actions are affected by worry or causing you worry. Don't panic, minor adjustments will help, so read on.

21-30 You certainly need to make adjustments to the way you are going about your life, because worry is reflected in your actions. Make sure you read on.

31-40 Your levels of worry are way too high. You deserve more than this out of life. You have been 'getting out of life' rather than 'getting into life' and you need to implement an action plan as soon as possible.

EMOTIONS/FEELINGS

Score each question	
Seldom/not much	O
Often/a fair bit	1
Almost all the time	2

I feel anxious and nervous _____

I feel uncertain and unsure _____

I feel sad, blue and depressed _____

I feel guilty, full of self-blame _____

My life feels out of control _____

Other people make me feel unhappy _____

I feel my head will explode _____

I feel unworthy and less than others _____

I feel physically sick _____

I feel irritable and moody _____

Score each question	
Seldom/not much	2
Often/a fair bit	1
Almost all the time	O

I feel happy and contented _____

I feel free to be myself _____

I feel relaxed and at ease _____

I feel in control of my life _____

I feel healthy and well _____

I am optimistic, hopeful about the future _____

I am loved by people close to me _____

I am a worthwhile and useful human being _____

I feel pleased with my achievements in life _____

I am not afraid of dying _____

Total score (out of 40) _____

If you scored:

0-10 You are pretty well in control. Your emotional state indicates little worry, keep it up.

11-20 You're on the borderline — some worry is popping into your emotional and feeling state. Have a close look at your score, that's where effort is needed.

21-30 You're a worrier alright. Emotions need pulling into line pretty smartly — that's what the rest of the book is for.

31-40 Please don't worry about your score! Many people will score here. The following chapters will help you turn your emotions back under your control. Your emotions are generally a direct reflection on your actions and attitudes, so read on.

WHAT DOES IT ALL MEAN?

Have a close look at your scores and then decide:

◆ where a lot of your worry comes from, and

◆ how worry pops out in you.

Now complete this little exercise.

It appears my worry comes from:

1. _____

2. _____

3. _____

4. _____

The way worry comes out in me is:

1. _____

2. _____

3. _____

4. _____

This exercise will help you understand and focus on the self-control techniques discussed later in the book, which will be most beneficial for you.

You will now have a fairly good idea if you worry too much, or if indeed worry is a concern for you and you need to do something about it. If your score is very low on the three checklists then read on. You are very much in control of worry, the trick is to stay that way, and the rest of the book will be useful to help you maintain your present state.

If you had rather high scores, then the coming chapters will help you to understand your worry habit and give you some useful and practical advice and techniques on how to reduce your habit and gain far more personal control.

SUMMARY

◆ We worry about pleasant events, not just unpleasant ones.
◆ Common things we worry about:
 happiness;
 health;
 future;
 work;
 money;
 relationships;
 marriage.
◆ We can literally worry about anything.
◆ Know what you worry about — use the checklist.
◆ We don't have to stop all worry.
◆ The only good worry is 'short' worry.
◆ We need to switch from *worry* to *solution*.
◆ Use checklists as a guide to 'too much worry'.
◆ Where does your worry appear to come from?
◆ How does worry pop out in you?
◆ If you have only a little worry, you need to maintain this.
◆ If a worry habit is present, it's time to take control.

CHAPTER 3

The effects of worrying

We have already been introduced to some of the effects of worry in the last chapter. However a slightly more in-depth consideration is necessary so that we fully understand how debilitating and damaging to ourselves worry can be.

Worry can be one of those things we treat a bit frivolously in life. In other words we take it a bit lightly, have a giggle about it and then perhaps smoke a packet of cigarettes, drink too much alcohol or yell at someone close to us, in our efforts to cope with it.

The effects of worry on individuals vary enormously. As we saw before, when some people worry about something they quickly switch the worry into more flexible and positive thinking, formulate an action plan and find a solution to whatever it was

they were worrying about. Others among us will deal with worry by just letting it drift on and interfering to varying degrees with their quality of life and their self-confidence.

And for far too many people, worry will come out in the form of major symptoms that severely interfere with their ability to lead a relaxed and fulfilling life.

CASE STUDY

Glenys, 45, had seen a psychologist and was told she was suffering from agoraphobia. She had been extremely worried and anxious whenever she had to go outside of her house — even to collect the mail from the letter box. The worry began when she thought about leaving the house and got worse as she started to leave the house. She had felt and been this way for 14 years. She felt extremely guilty about the fact that her husband did the shopping. Glenys resisted going to any social functions because she was frightened she might have a panic attack (overwhelming anxiety, pounding heart, dizziness) when she was out, so she stayed indoors. There had not been a panic attack for four and a half years, yet she avoided situations because she worried that if she did have an attack, she would make a fool of herself.

So what can be the effects of worry? Of course, these will differ from person to person.

Tick any of the following signs or symptoms of worry that may indicate how worry is affecting you.

Physical		Psychological	
muscle tension	_____	poor sleep	_____
nausea	_____	irritable	_____
diarrhoea or constipation	_____	frequent crying	_____
skin rashes	_____	anxiety	_____
frowning	_____	depressed	_____

SORTING OUT WORRY

stomach pains	_____	withdrawal/avoidance	_____
eating too much/little	_____	low self-esteem	_____
nervous tics	_____		
grinding teeth	_____		
shaking/trembling	_____		
stuttering			

Physiological (tick if yes)		**Emotional** (tick if yes)	
high blood pressure	_____	frequent crying	_____
racing heart	_____	angry outbursts	_____
dry mouth	_____	sadness	_____
breathing quickly	_____	exhaustion	_____
light-headed	_____		

Interpersonal (interaction with others) (tick if yes)

self-conscious	_____	offish	_____
uptight/on edge	_____	bragging	_____
passive	_____	poor eye contact	_____
lonely	_____		

So how did you fare? If you have ticked a number of symptoms that you can remember experiencing, then it is likely that worry is a problem or potential problem for you. Especially if you scored fairly highly on the previous checklists. Let's consider some of those symptoms and signs of worry in more detail.

MUSCLE TENSIONS

Muscles commonly affected by worry include those in the head, shoulder, chest, stomach and lower back. Tension may be experienced as stiffness, aches, pains or sore spots.

BOWEL PROBLEMS

Diarrhoea and constipation can be common signs of worry. Anxiety before a sporting event or any important event in our lives may find us rushing to the toilet a number of times before the event. Worry also seems to play a part in irritable bowel syndrome, which can also result in stomach problems.

DEPRESSION

Thoughts of hopelessness and helplessness can occur if worry builds within us. A sense of sadness may overwhelm us. We believe we are being punished, and there is a feeling of being a failure. We may feel that life is barely worth the effort. Events lose their enjoyment and negative thoughts persist.

EATING PATTERNS

Worry can lead to a marked change in food intake and eating habits. Mild to moderate amounts of worry often see an increase in our intake, almost as a comforting phenomenon — we feel full and contented. Severe worry, when it results in anxiety and panic, can be associated with a marked decrease in food intake and hence weight loss.

INSOMNIA (SLEEP PROBLEMS)

This is a very common sign of worry. Sleep is generally one of the first things to be affected along with our ability to concentrate. Sleep may be affected by:

◆ an inability to fall asleep within 20 minutes;

◆ frequent waking during the night; or

◆ early awakening and inability to get back to sleep.

We generally become aware of the 'racing mind syndrome' which consists of worrying thoughts running endlessly over and over in our mind.

ANXIETY DISORDERS

Anxiety disorders, from mild to severe, are generally associated with worry. Following are some of the anxiety disorders associated with varying degrees of worry:

◆ generalised anxiety disorder — this is feeling frequently anxious and uptight due to an established worry habit that we have fallen into;

◆ simple phobia — this is where worry and fear are associated with one particular thing, such as snakes, spiders, confined spaces or heights.

◆ social phobia — this is worry about being in crowded places or mixing with a group of people.

◆ agoraphobia (panic and avoidance) — this can be a very debilitating condition associated with leaving a 'safe' place such as your home. There is the worry that we might have a panic attack (intense fear, pounding heart, faintness, breathlessness) and so collapse, make a fool of ourselves, die or go mad.

◆ alcohol/drugs — the use of alcohol or prescribed or illegal drugs is often the result of trying to rid ourselves of worry. What often happens of course is that the amount of drugs or alcohol being consumed becomes a problem in itself and can also lead to other problems such as violence or ill-health.

◆ loneliness — we may isolate ourselves from others if we feel we are not as good at things, as smart or attractive as others. We may worry ourselves into embarrassment or low self-esteem and so miss the support and friendship that comes from socialising and mixing with others.

CAUTION

So worry is not something to be taken lightly. It may result in or exacerbate conditions which can severely interfere with our quality of life. If the worry persists, the conditions often persist. Some depressive and anxiety disorders may become clinical disorders and require professional help from a clinical psychologist.

Feeling confident about dealing with worry is crucial if we wish to experience a fulfilling life, and be capable of enjoying the many marvellous experiences and journeys life has to offer. For some, worry will lead to a severe depressive disorder and suicide — this is indeed most unfortunate and unnecessary. Few of the things we worry about are catastrophes or even major life events. There are *always* solutions and other ways of dealing with situations that may seem hopeless. Remember that just because we feel hopeless does not mean we are. It is only our perception of things. Perceptions are often driven by our feelings, not by reality. When we take control of our feelings by changing our attitudes and behaviour we find far more positive and adaptive solutions to the worries in our life.

SUMMARY

◆ Be vigilant, not frivolous, about worry.

◆ Effects on individuals vary enormously.

◆ Check for any signs or symptoms of worry.

◆ There is a need to feel confident in dealing with worry.

◆ Beware of feelings. Try to change attitudes and behaviour.

◆ Positive and adaptive solutions are a reality.

CHAPTER 4

Why do we worry?

It's time to consider that inevitable question, 'why do we worry?' It's interesting to consider how often we say to ourselves 'it was no big deal, I don't know what I was worried about'. And yet we were certainly worried — frowning, tense, sullen and snappy. If at times we can see things very clearly, keep them in perspective and move on, why don't we tend to do this more often and nip the worry in the bud? In other words, why do we have so much trouble taking common sense into common practice?

Habit!

As I have stated before, worry can become a habit in the same way other positive or not so positive human actions and attitudes become routine and habit. Human beings find it quite difficult to break patterns of behaviours and specific thinking styles (attitudes and beliefs that they develop over time). This is because we tend to put our habits on *automatic pilot* and let them fly by themselves. Unfortunately we seldom troubleshoot these habits by flying ourselves on *manual* for a while, analysing what we are doing, and making any repairs or changes in our habit patterns that might be necessary.

Apart from habit, particular *crises* in our lives can also bring on worry. Life may have been going along fairly predictably and smoothly. We may have sensed and felt a good level of control over our immediate and longer-term destiny. Then something unpredictable occurs, perhaps something that we feel is uncon-

trollable, and we throw ourselves into a state of turmoil fuelled by worry. The turmoil and worry then feed on themselves to ensure we do indeed experience a crisis!

CASE STUDY

Kate, 43, was leading a very active life as a wife and mother, with a career in banking. She was also a keen sportswoman. The discovery, by herself, of a lump in her breast threw her life into turmoil. By the time she plucked up the courage to see her doctor, she had convinced herself it was malignant. She could not concentrate at work, stopped her sporting activities and became preoccupied with ensuring her family would be looked after following her death. Kate became withdrawn, irritable and tearful around her family. Her family knew nothing of the lump.

Eventually overcome by the worry and feeling exhausted, Kate made a doctor's appointment. The doctor's opinion was confirmed by a mammogram one day later; a benign growth, no need for any intervention. The only threat to Kate's well-being was the worry!

So why do we worry? Why do we make mountains out of molehills, get things out of perspective and generally give ourselves a hard time? There are a few reasons:

CONDITIONING/UPBRINGING

The experiences we are exposed to in our younger years will have a marked effect on the way we react to things later in life. If we grow up in a family environment where concern, uncertainty and worry are commonplace, it is likely we will develop similar traits and ways of thinking about and running our lives. So if our parents, in particular, were worriers, it is likely we will have developed similar traits. Worry is most certainly a learned habit.

GENETICS/BIOLOGY

There is no convincing evidence that worry is transported through our genetic make up. The argument that 'I was born a worrier' is no more than a very flimsy excuse, not backed up by the research. At this stage we know from the research that worry can be learned, but we are still unsure of the role our genetic make up plays. Even if there is a genetic component, evidence is clear that we can break the worry cycle and unfreeze the habit.

SURVIVAL

Worry, as we have already seen, can serve a very useful purpose if:

◆ it is short in duration, and

◆ is focused on potentially dangerous issues.

Being focused on potential danger or harm for a short time may help us to take appropriate action to avoid injury or perhaps death. Theorists who believe in evolution would see this as something built into us to assist with the survival of the species. That is, if we can avoid danger or alert ourselves to it quickly, more of us will survive to go on and produce more of us!

OURSELVES AND OUR BELIEFS

Individually, *we* are the major reason that we worry. This can be difficult for some of us to understand. Most concern and anxiety about events in life is due to the way we interpret our perceptions about what is happening in our world. We develop, from a host of sources and for a range of reasons, a memory bank full of the way things in our lives should be, or must go, if they are seen to be okay. Then, when things don't go as planned, a common occurrence, we use beliefs from our memory banks to worry about them, sometimes a great deal. The beliefs stored in the belief system in our memory are things like 'I must be loved by everyone if I am to be worthwhile', 'I must/should never make a mistake if I am to be okay', 'I must/should get very upset when others have problems'.

In fact a psychologist, Dr Albert Ellis, has found at least ten irrational beliefs that individuals regularly develop and store in that belief system in their memory. These can lead to a great deal of worry. Those beliefs are:

1. I must be loved, or at least liked, and approved by every significant person I meet.
2. I must be completely competent, make no mistakes, and achieve in every possible way, if I am to be worthwhile.
3. Some people are bad, wicked, or evil, and they should be blamed and punished for this.
4. It is dreadful, it's nearly the end of the world, when things aren't how I would like them to be.

5. Human unhappiness, including mine, is caused by factors outside of my control, so little can be done about it.
6. If something might be dangerous, unpleasant or frightening, I should worry about it a great deal.
7. It's easier to put off something difficult or unpleasant than it is to face up to it.
8. I need someone stronger than myself to depend on.
9. My problem(s) were caused by event(s) in my past, and that's why I have my problem(s) now.
10. I should be very upset by other people's problems and difficulties.

Before we move on, let's take some time and see if any of those types of beliefs apply to us. They may not be as extreme as written above, but do we have thoughts and actions which may indicate that those beliefs lead to a little, or a great amount of worry for ourselves?

Think back over the last few weeks and the various events and activities in your life both of a personal and work nature. Are you now, or do you remember, feeling anxious, worried or concerned for a reasonable period of time about anything in particular?

I felt anxious, worried or concerned about:

Situation 1. _____

2. _____

3. _____

4. _____

Now relate those experiences to the irrational beliefs we have just read about. Can you identify one or a number which were behind your worry, concern or anxiety? If so, note them down now as something to be aware of — we will deal with them in later chapters.

Irrational beliefs involved in the situations listed by you:

1. _____

2. _____

3. _____

4. _____

ARE THESE BELIEFS IRRATIONAL?

Why are these types of beliefs irrational, especially since so many of us possess so many of them?

They are irrational because there is no universal law or scientific evidence that says we *should* or *must* do or have these things. There certainly is no evidence to support that fact that we indeed could, even if we wanted to. What we have done, if we have any or a number of those beliefs, is to have taken our preferences in life, that is our wish to be loved, be right all the time and have things our way, and turned them into absolute shoulds or musts. We say things to ourselves like 'I should always . . .' or 'I must always . . .'.

We set ourselves up to worry a great deal about things in life which are absolutely impossible to achieve. We set unrealistic goals for ourselves and/or others and then worry, get angry, upset, anxious or blaming when they do not occur. It's interesting how unintelligently we can think as human beings. I guess it just goes to show that we are all fallible after all. It's okay to be fallible and make mistakes. If we want to correct our worry habit, it's not okay to ignore these errors in the way we think. We need to work on correcting them. Where did they come from? Many certainly would have come from our upbringing. Others from general influences in socialising with others who also have many irrational beliefs. Some people may have a biological predisposition to think that way. However, the major contributor to continuing and forming a thinking pattern or irrational *belief system* is ourselves.

To begin to turn those irrational beliefs into more rational beliefs and so ease our worry and anxiety we need to understand where these types of beliefs are located and how they are activated by events in our lives. Why do some people have more irrational beliefs than others? Why do we all tend to react differently to the same event in life? Why do some people experience intense worry and concern when they think about death for example, and yet others feel quite relaxed, calm and accepting?

CASE STUDY

David and Maria had been holidaying in the United States for 10 days. It had been a wonderful experience and both had enjoyed everything about their first overseas trip. On their way home they stayed one night in Honolulu. The next day when they rang to confirm their flight home, they were told a 24 hour strike by the airline's pilots meant they would have to spend another day in Hawaii. The airline would pay for the extra accommodation and an evening meal at their hotel. Maria was delighted, but David was angry and upset, saying things like 'the airlines shouldn't allow this to happen, it's the last time I fly with this airline, it's wrecked the whole holiday'.

The same situation, two totally different reactions — why does this happen? The next chapter will help us understand why.

SUMMARY

◆ Worry can become a *habit*.

◆ A crisis in our lives can lead to ongoing worry.

◆ Why do we worry?
conditioning/upbringing;
genetics/biology;
ourselves and our beliefs.

◆ Beware of the ten common irrational beliefs.

◆ There are no universal laws or scientific evidence to support those irrational beliefs.

◆ Why do we all tend to react differently to the same sort of events in life?

CHAPTER 5

Making sense of it all

Understanding why you worry, or how you learned to worry, will not generally stop the habit, but it will help you to understand the next chapter, which explains how to control your worry. In the meantime, let's try to make a little more sense of this phenomenon called worry.

Imagine you are sitting at the kitchen table and a large red-bellied black snake slithers in through the kitchen door! Your reaction would no doubt be to fall backwards off the chair and make for the nearest exit feeling quite panicky. However, had it been a bush tucker man sitting at the table and the same red-bellied black snake slithered in through the door, there would be a totally different reaction. Chances are he may walk towards the reptile, pick it up by the tail, pop it into a bag and probably cook it in a bush oven for dinner that night!

Although this is a somewhat extreme example, I feel it does highlight what I am getting at. There were two totally different reactions to the same situation. Why? Why doesn't the same

situation, in this case the appearance of a snake, cause the same
concern and worry in all of us?
Well, it has to do with that *tape
recorder* in your head. I will
explain about the tape recorder
and its role in your worry. First,
however, we have to go back a
step or two. The three time periods surrounding any event in life
are important — *before* the
event, *during* the event, and *after*
the event.

Sometimes *before* an event you get time to worry about it in
anticipation, at other times, situations arise unexpectedly.

During the event is fairly self-explanatory, and *after* the
event is very important as it can play a big part in how you
react to the next event, especially a similar one. If, following an
event, we feel anxious, worried or upset, then we are likely to
feel that way again when a similar event is about to happen.

CASE STUDY

Julie, 37, had her first job interview in eight years. Her youngest
child had just started primary school and Julie had decided to
return to work. She was a qualified accountant. When first told
of her interview for the job Julie was ecstatic. Two days before
the interview she was a nervous wreck — she was apprehensive,
couldn't sleep and was nauseous. She had begun to worry about
the interview — 'am I too old? will I cope back at work? will I
remember the basics? is this really what I want to do?' She was
literally beginning to worry herself sick.

Now, from any event in our life (before, during or after) there
will be consequences for us, and these consequences will have

an impact on our behaviour (actions), our thinking (attitudes and beliefs) and our emotions (feelings and moods). If a pleasant event happens, we will act, think and feel happy. If a negative event occurs, we may act, think and feel quite depressed.

EVENT
BEFORE
DURING
AFTER

CONSEQUENCES
BEHAVIOUR-THINKING-EMOTIONS
(ACTIONS-ATTITUDES-FEELINGS)

However, as we found with the snake example, the same event can have totally different consequences for different people. Why? How you react to any event in your life is dependent on what you have stored on the tape recorder in your head which I mentioned at the beginning of this chapter.

Now, I want you to imagine that up in your head you have a tape recorder with a tape in it. The tape contains your memory banks. All those experiences from your past, your present circumstances and your expectations of the future are stored on that tape in the form of memories, that is, everything that got through to your long-term memory. From all this information you have developed attitudes, beliefs, values, judgments and perceptions about what life is all about and how it 'should' and 'must' be. The information stored on your tape is sometimes referred to as a *belief system*. Remember in the last chapter I spoke about those ten popular irrational beliefs we can acquire during our lives.

OUR MEMORY BANK
Belief System

Before	TAPE RECORDER	Consequences
During	Memory Banks	Behaviour-Thoughts-Emotions
$\longrightarrow$	$\longrightarrow$	
After	(Belief System)	(Actions)(Attitudes/Beliefs)(Feelings)

An event is about to happen, is happening or has just happened and 'switches on' the tape in your head which then plays you messages about the event. Now, what comes out of the tape recorder will depend on what is stored on the tape. This in turn, will affect the consequences for us in terms of our behaviour, ongoing thoughts and emotions. If positive attitudes and beliefs are released, the consequences will be positive. If negative and irrational beliefs and judgments are made, the consequences for us, in terms of our behaviour, ongoing thoughts and emotions are likely to be quite negative, such as worry, anxiety and uncertainty. So what, or who, determines what goes into our belief systems? As I have already mentioned, it often starts with your parents, the values and beliefs they demonstrated at home, then your peers, school teachers, work mates — literally all your experiences throughout life are included in the formation of your belief system. You then form these into ways of making judgments about things in your life. You form values, expectations and decide how your world should, or must be if you are to feel okay.

You can imagine how many beliefs involving worries, uncertainties and fears are stored on your tape, often stemming from one of those ten irrational beliefs we are already aware of.

These beliefs are often stored in the 'what if?' section of the tape:

◆ what if I make a mistake?
◆ what if I can't cope?
◆ what if he/she does not like me?
◆ what if my business fails?
◆ what if I don't come first?

◆ what if I'm not a perfect parent?

There will probably be many 'worry' sections on your tape. Many of these you may not be aware of at this time, however they will be having quite an impact on your overall quality of life. When your tape contains too many worries, too many uncertainties, too many fears or anxieties, there is literally not enough room for growth-inducing positive beliefs which will enhance your overall lifestyle and help you adapt to and enjoy the challenges through your life.

Quite often when events are about to happen, are happening or have just happened, we are unaware of what messages (beliefs) are coming out of the tape recorder, and the impact of those messages on us. It is as though we are going through life on automatic pilot with our mind in cruise mode. At other times you may be well aware of the messages from your tape, and what effects they are having on you.

It's time to dissect our belief systems! In Chapter 4 we began the process by considering some recent experiences which we may have reacted to with worry, uncertainty or anxiety. We then listed down which of the ten popular irrational beliefs we felt may have led to our state of apprehension.

Now I want you to think even more generally and list four recent events; the messages you feel came out of your tape recorder about those events and the impact they had on you in terms of your behaviour and your emotions (feelings/mood).

Events ⟶	Messages/beliefs from your tape recorder ⟶	Impact/ consequences for you
1._____	_____	_____
2._____	_____	_____
3._____	_____	_____
4._____	_____	_____

By analysing those events and the messages you were giving

yourself about them, were you able to get an idea about some of the beliefs and attitudes you may have stored on the tape in that tape recorder? It is important to begin focusing on how those thoughts led to you acting in a particular way. Were they very pessimistic or optimistic in their nature? Is it easy to see how they led to worry, continued it, or in fact stopped you worrying?

Beginning to understand the role of our thoughts and belief systems in terms of the effects they have on our behaviour is not only important, but can be rather exciting. It means we do have the power to control our reactions to things.

By ridding ourselves of beliefs which are worrying or can lead to worry, we can alter the way we perceive events in life and our reactions to them. We can begin to control what attitudes and beliefs we store in our tape recorder.

We can begin to see that it is no one else or nothing else that gets us upset, anxious or worried, but rather we get ourselves upset by what we are saying to ourselves about things. As we saw in the last chapter, if we use absolute 'shoulds' or 'musts' such as 'I should always' or 'you must always', we are setting ourselves up to fail. We are setting ourselves up to worry and get anxious because we cannot possibly live up to those unrealistic expectations. We are human and we are fallible.

We most certainly need to give life our very best shot, and every now and then we will mess up, make a mistake or do something silly. So what? What can happen? Will the world end? No! You may be a little embarrassed, perhaps sorry, but you will have learned something. Most things that happen are not catastrophes and we seldom totally lose the plot. In the next chapter we begin to look at how to keep things in perspective and how to develop and control our belief system.

SUMMARY

◆ Similar events bring different reactions from different people.

◆ We can and do get worried *before*, *during*, and *after* an event.

◆ Consequences and events in our lives will have an effect on our behaviour, thinking and emotions.

◆ We have a *belief system* stored in the tape recorder in our head.

◆ Life experiences influence what goes onto the tape in our tape recorder.

◆ Beware of the 'what if?' syndrome.

◆ Belief systems can operate on automatic pilot.

◆ Be careful about catastrophising things.

◆ Beliefs and attitudes lead to certain behaviour or actions.

◆ We can control what attitudes and beliefs we store in the tape recorder.

CHAPTER 6

Taking control — controlling your attitudes and beliefs

By now you should understand how important *thinking*, *attitudes* and *beliefs* are in the whole worrying saga. So how do you get, and keep, control over your thoughts and thinking processes and hence your actions, which may fuel your worries or concerns? The answer is the same way you gain control over anything else in your life. You *practise* what it is you wish to be good at.

You know that you must practise forehands and backhands if you wish to play tennis well, you know that you must play your scales if you wish to play the piano well. However, you may not understand what and how to practise if you want to stop worrying. What can you do about that tape recorder, belief system and the resultant worries and concerns, and their impact on your lifestyle? You need to take control of the whole process — and you can. Control the tape recorder! Control what goes on the tape! Change the worry, concern or fear messages and beliefs on the tape which you consider do not contribute to your quality of life.

The reality is that taking control is not that difficult. All it takes is desire and know-how. Here are some very practical techniques to help you gain control of your own belief system.

No matter how old (and wise?) you may be, what job position you hold, or your IQ score, some of the beliefs in your belief system will be:

- inflexible — 'of course it's a worry';
- rigid — 'I've always been a worrier';
- irrational — 'I should worry about that a great deal, it's a catastrophe';
- negative — 'what if I look foolish? This shouldn't happen to me';
- upsetting — 'I can't stand to think about it'.

One or a number of these beliefs can be a major source of stress, unproductive behaviour and upsetting emotional reactions.

Don't panic, you have survived your 'worrying belief system' up to this time, so many of those beliefs you have stored up in that tape are:

- Flexible — 'what are all the facts involved?';
- Adaptable — 'is there another way which may work?';
- Rational — 'no shoulds or musts';
- Positive — 'I can if I put my mind to it';
- Solution-oriented — 'what is the best thing for me to do right now?'

There is no room for debilitating worries in that part of your belief system, only a positive, solution-orientation to whatever situations or events are presenting themselves.

This is good quality thinking which works well for any situation in life.

The answer to taking control of your tape recorder and belief system and hence getting rid of the cause of many of your so called worries is hopefully becoming clearer. You need to *stop* that tape recorder whenever any worrying or upsetting beliefs begin to appear, and switch your thinking to become more flexible, adaptable, rational, positive and solution-orientated.

The best way to do this is to imagine that you *stop* the tape in your head and tape FARPS beliefs over those old worries, concerns and anxiety provoking beliefs. The technique you use to do this is easiest thought of as a *thought stopping and thought switching technique*. Here's how it goes:

Place a reasonably sturdy, comfortably fitting rubber band on one of your wrists.

Now let's say you are about to go for a job interview and you find yourself apprehensive, irritable and thinking 'what if I don't do as well as I had hoped, I'll feel a real fool, I'm not looking forward to this!'

Step 1 — Grab the rubber band and give yourself a gentle flick on the wrist. The rubber band is there to remind you to be aware of what that tape recorder in your head is doing. The flick on the wrist is to make you aware of what you are saying to yourself from your belief system.

Step 2 — Imagine a *stop* sign coming up in front of your face and gently yell the word 'stop' to yourself in your head (self-talk).

The idea, of course, is to stop the tape recorder and those worrying beliefs playing on and on.

Step 3 — Now 'switch' your thinking and beliefs to become more flexible, adaptable, rational, positive and solution-oriented. To do this, just imagine a switch clicking from one side to the other as you change your thinking across.

Step 4 — Tape over those worrying and negative beliefs, those 'what ifs' with four or five positive and solution-oriented self-talks', such as:

◆ 'Hey! relax, calm down';

◆ 'This is not a life threatening situation';

◆ 'I will give it my best shot, and that will be good enough this time';

◆ 'I don't have anything to prove to anyone';

◆ 'Good on me for taking control of my beliefs'.

So, in abbreviated form, this is what the thought stopping and thought switching technique looks like:

◆ imagine a *stop* sign in front of your face and yell 'stop' to yourself;

◆ switch your thinking to 'FARPS':

    flexible,
    adaptable,
    rational,
    positive,
    solution-oriented;

◆ positive self-talk — four or five short statements.

What you have now started to do is to take control and ownership over those *beliefs* and messages on your tape which have been a major source of worry for you. You really have started to say that 'I will control my beliefs and attitudes about events in my life. I will not be a victim to negative, irrational and stress-inducing perceptions about aspects of my life'. Refuse to be part of the Victim Trap or 'poor me' trap.

Remember that the beliefs in that tape recorder were learned. With practice you can learn to tape new positive beliefs over those which caused, and still may cause, you to feel worried. Remember also that your attitudes and beliefs about events and happenings in your life will very much influence your behaviour (actions) and your emotions (moods). However, your behaviour or actions in the face of worry may also need some assistance. In a later chapter we will look at a problem-solving technique to help replace those self-defeating actions with positive actions. We need to build up our positive and solution-oriented belief system that we have learned to control and influence in that tape recorder in our head.

PRACTISE, PRACTISE, PRACTISE

How are we going to make sure that we get to a point where we feel confident in using the thought stopping and thought switch technique? How can we ensure that it will work quickly and effectively for us? Like anything else in life, the answer is through practice.

The following exercise is to help you practise by focusing specifically on:
1. what is happening;
2. what you can do about it, and
3. the benefits for you at the end of it all.

This technique was initially the work of Dr Albert Ellis, the psychologist I mentioned earlier in the book. Research has shown it to be extremely successful in helping people gain control over worry, anxiety and depressive disorders. Use the actual example to follow, or photocopy it and enlarge it if you wish. You may also rewrite the method on a pad to use for future situations. The procedure to practise is:

Example
1. *Identify the situation of concern*:
   Teenage daughter half an hour late home from a party.
2. *Irrational and upsetting self-talk (beliefs)*

43

She should consider us more. She probably had an accident. She is totally irresponsible. I shouldn't have let her go.

3. *Actions resulting from irrational thoughts*:
   Sleeplessness
   Pacing the floor
   Cup after cup of coffee

   Emotions resulting from irrational thoughts:
   Anger
   Anxiety
   Fear

4. *Disputing upsetting beliefs, that is, more flexible, adaptable, rational, positive and solution-orientated attitudes — FARPS-ing*:
   She is a mature, sensible girl.
   I will talk to her about our concerns in the morning.
   It's okay for me to feel a little concern, but acting out a drama will not help.

5. Effects of FARPS — disputing irrational/upsetting beliefs:

Actions/behaviours:	*Beliefs/attitudes*:	*Emotions/feelings*:
– Sleep	– She is only half an hour late	– More relaxed
– Discuss the issue next morning	– I can discuss this rationally	– Little anxiety – In control
– Treat teenager as sensible and mature	– My worry will not help at all	– Pleasant

Now it's your turn.

1. Identify the situation of concern

_____

_____

_____

2. Irrational and upsetting beliefs

_____

_____

_____

3. Actions resulting from   Emotions resulting from
beliefs/thoughts   beliefs/thoughts

_____   _____

_____   _____

_____   _____

4. Disputing upsetting beliefs, that is, more flexible, adaptable,
rational, positive and solution-orientated attitudes — FARPSing

_____

_____

_____

5. Effects of disputing irrational/upsetting beliefs (FARPS)

   actions/behaviour   beliefs/attitudes   emotions/feelings

   _____   _____   _____

   _____   _____   _____

   _____   _____   _____

As the saying goes, 'practice makes perfect', and the benefits
are enormous. You will have a greater sense of :

◆ personal control;

◆ positive focus;

◆ higher self-esteem;

◆ fulfilment;

◆ happiness;

◆ contentedness;

◆ control of your own destiny.

And of course all these benefits condense into one major personal
gain — less worry.

While this technique may seem or appear to be common sense, we cannot assume that automatically we will think or perceive situations this rationally.

So make sure you are very adept at remaining positive and solution-orientated. The benefits are not only there for yourself, but for all those around you. Others will see a person who is more relaxed, more fun, more rational, more optimistic and more self-assured. Try it — it works.

CASE STUDY

Judy, a 43 year old mother of three children, was a chronic worrier. One of the issues that concerned her was the role of mother. She felt that because her children had been in pre-school while she went to work, that they had suffered in some fashion. By working through the process of rational thinking described above, Judy was able to dispute those irrational beliefs and gain an insight into her 'worries'. When she began to dispute beliefs such as 'my children were deprived, I neglected my children', Judy replaced those with more rational beliefs such as 'my children learnt how to socialise, they were in a very stimulating environment'. For the first time in many years she let go of the worry and began to see herself as a very responsible mother who had ensured her children had very good care during those years. She then began to apply this technique to other areas of her life.

SUMMARY

◆ Remember to use FARPS beliefs and attitudes.

◆ Practise a thought stopping and thought switching technique.

◆ Practise the FARPS beliefs using the method described in this chapter.

◆ Personal benefits are many.

◆ You owe it to yourself.

CHAPTER 7

Taking control — techniques and ideas

We need to concentrate on controlling our attitudes and beliefs about these things which occur, or which we feel may occur, in our lives. If we don't, we will never be in control of gaining the most out of life and breaking any form of *worry habit* that we may have developed.

Here's a hint. When attempting any of these techniques remember that *ability* is not enough, what you need is *stickability*, to put some effort and energy into making sure that your ability is maximised and that positive habits are developed.

Keeping things in perspective is a crucial ability in terms of

stopping worry and also in being able to maintain a rational attitude towards all things that are happening, and will happen, in our lives. So how do we keep things in perspective? Is there a reasonably easy and straightforward way of doing this? What about when one thing happens after another, and irrational thoughts, emotions and actions seem to take over, almost automatically? Can we do anything about this? And what about making 'mountains out of molehills' when we look back and ask why we bothered?

There is something we can do and many of us would already have been using this technique or something similar. This technique was once again pioneered by Dr Albert Ellis the author of *How to Stubbornly Refuse to Make Yourself Miserable*. It is a great idea and very sound advice, so let's see how it works.

THE CATASTROPHE SCALE

This technique is called the *catastrophe scale*. It is a fairly straightforward technique and is aimed at keeping things in perspective. The way to remember how to use the scale is to form mental pictures or imagery. The illustrations will assist you with this. The easiest way to think about the catastrophe scale is to imagine it as a small ruler sitting up there in your head. The ruler is marked or calibrated from 0–100.

In terms of a catastrophe in life, 10 on the scale is something minor, 25 would be a pain, 50 is something quite serious, 75 is getting reasonably more serious and 90 is something pretty traumatic. Now think about something in life that is pretty traumatic in reality! You will probably come up with things like the death of someone close to you, being made a quadriplegic in a road accident, or the diagnosis of a terminal illness. These things would rate about 90–99 on the scale. In reality then, retrenchment from a job or your house burning down would rate 50–75 compared with death and terminal illness. Dropping a plate in the kitchen would, in comparison, rate 2. So the picture so far looks like this:

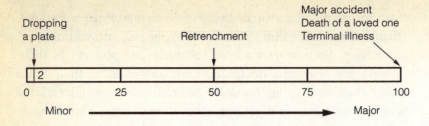

Most things that happen to us on a day to day basis probably rate from 2–20 in reality. However if we do not keep things in perspective, our reactions to these everyday happenings could be up to around the 90 mark.

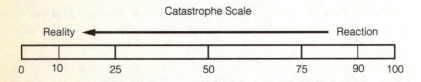

The idea then, is to quickly remind ourselves that the reality of what is happening is around 10 out of 100. We then bring our *reaction* back to a rating of 10 also. We calm down, keep things in perspective and forget the exaggerating.

To stop the catastrophising thoughts, use the thought stopping and thought switching technique we learnt in the last chapter. When you realise that you are exaggerating things and getting yourself tense, flick yourself gently with the rubber band, say the word 'stop' to yourself, then *switch* your thinking to FARPS and say four or five rational self-talks to yourself — 'Relax I can cope with this, I'm just blowing it out of proportion, where does it sit on the catastrophe scale, its no big deal, what's the best thing to do'.

This is not difficult, but it often needs a little practice. One of the most important things of course, is to remember to do it, and to do it regularly so it becomes a habit — something we tend to do automatically. I am sure you will find this technique very useful and reasonably simple to use. Remember that practice makes for positive habits, so keep at it.

To assist us in being able to recognise those things we tend to let get out of perspective, let's spend a few moments considering what those things are:

Things I regularly blow out of perspective
Examples: How important an issue is.
How dreadful someone has been to me.

_____

_____

_____

_____

_____

Sometimes we have to think about it a little, but they are there, and it can be a useful self-discovery process. Once we have pin-pointed what these fairly common loss of perspective things are, it is far easier to remember to be aware, and pull ourselves up, if we are tending to slip into them. Now, from the list of things that you tend to allow to get out of perspective, what are two that you are going to focus on and use the catastrophe scale to help keep them far more in perspective?

Keep a close eye on:

_____

_____

_____

_____

_____

To help us understand what we have actually done in starting to control our thinking and attitudes more, let's liken the process to an aircraft. When an aircraft is airborne and flying to its destination it is generally placed on automatic pilot by the captain. We're much the same. When going about our everyday

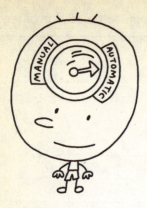

life and business we place our thinking and attitudes on automatic and just cruise through life with our brain and past experience running us, often unaware of what we are thinking and what our attitudes are.

When we decide we have had enough of the worry habit, and begin to use the thought stopping and thought switching technique and the catastrophe scale to start enjoying life and relaxing more, what we are doing is switching the automatic pilot off and flying ourselves on *manual*. We need to do this for a while to fix up those maladaptive attitudes. We are actually telling the brain what to do and filling that tape recorder with flexible, adaptable, rational, positive and solution-orientated thinking.

Once we feel more in control and find that we are able to keep things far more in perspective, we can then switch ourselves back onto automatic pilot. We then place ourselves back on manual from time to time to check up that we are still doing well, seeing events in our lives as challenges, rather than terrible, awful major problems.

FOCUSING

A psychological technique that assists greatly with controlling the worry habit, helps us get things back in perspective and enhances our self-esteem, is one known as *focusing*. It is closely linked to the techniques we have already been exposed to, and I will now run through how to use it specifically for worry.

One of the things that constantly amazes me in life is how quick we are to kick our own backsides for something that we have done wrong, couldn't do, or believed we weren't smart enough to do. We then fill ourselves up with guilt and self-blame, destroy our own self-esteem, lose our confidence and begin to worry about everything and anything. Do we really mess up that often, do things so poorly and are as hopeless as we can lead ourselves to believe? No! Then why do we feel that way if it's generally not correct?

It's because we focus so readily on *what we can't do and what we haven't done* in life and we literally forget or overlook focusing on *what we can do and what we have done*.

We all do it, and if we do it too often we're in deep worry trouble. The answer is pretty clear. Many of you will probably only need to read this to gain some awareness. Others may need to practise *focusing*. You should, by now, have a fairly good idea of what focusing is all about. It requires us to concentrate on, and think about, all those things — small and large — that we do well throughout our normal day and during our journey through life. So let's get the negative focus out of the way first up. We need to do this next exercise so we can more easily detect when our focus has become distorted towards the negatives. Use the exercise to list as many of your *negative focuses* as you can. List the things you worry and focus on in the present and from your past. Include any negative focuses you may also have regarding your future.

My negative 'what I haven't done/can't do' focuses are:

Past	Present	Future
_____	_____	_____
_____	_____	_____
_____	_____	_____
_____	_____	_____

Add to these if you think of any more as we continue. I doubt that you had to think for long or dig very deep to find them. We often unearth quite a few once we start to become aware of them. Now, let's get constructive and positively focused. Use this part of the exercise to build a solid foundation for future focusing, that is, what do you do well and what you have done well. Remember that the everyday little things are just as important as the larger things. Do not leave out things just because you expect them of yourself. Include everything you can on the list, such as your neat and tidy appearance, your manners etc.

My positive focuses 'I can do/I have done' are:

Past	Present	Future
_____	_____	_____
_____	_____	_____
_____	_____	_____

You will probably be surprised at how many you had forgotten about. If you haven't come up with a pretty impressive list, you also probably need to read the book *Sorting Out Self-Esteem*, also in this series. Don't despair — grab someone you know well right now, or in the very near future, and get that person to give you a hand to complete the list. Keep the list as specific as possible.

Now for the crunch. You now need to make a determined pact with yourself that from this very moment in time onwards, you are going to focus on those things that you have done and that you can do. You must build on those things, so that you guide yourself towards the things in life that you wish to accomplish and achieve. If you lose the focus, and of course you will from time to time, no big deal, draw your focus and attention back to those things you can do, and have done well and run them through your tape recorder a few times to store them away for later. Make a list of those things you do well and carry it with you in your wallet or purse. A quick *checklist* can sometimes save a lot of worry and unnecessary anxiety because we can easily get to it and quickly read through it to help us *re-focus*.

This is another one of those easy to use techniques which help us take *common sense into common practice*. All the knowledge, education and ability in the world is worth absolutely nothing to us unless we use it in a very practical and regular manner for ourselves. Focusing is very strongly linked to self-esteem. When we focus positively we feel positive, when we focus poorly, we feel poorly. The choice is yours. Choose wisely!

QUICK RELAXATION TECHNIQUE

Now that we are becoming fairly adept at keeping things in perspective in order to reduce our worry, we need to take a little time to relax. Psychologically, relaxation is extremely important. The research carried out over a long time shows many benefits, not the least of which is our increased ability to think clearer and make better decisions. Other benefits include a change in brain waves, a healthier amount of adrenalin released into the body and a more efficient immune system.

I am really convinced that relaxation can cement in place our focus on keeping things in perspective, so we can take these positive and solution-orientated attitudes into positive actions and goal setting for ourselves. The quick relaxation technique I am about to introduce can be done regularly throughout the day. It is designed to last from two to ten minutes, and is best done in a comfortable chair with your eyes closed. However, parts of the technique can be used walking to a 'worrying' meeting, or driving to an appointment you are late for.

The technique goes like this:

— Get yourself comfortable, loosen any tight clothing, remove glasses.

— When comfortable, close your eyes begin to let your muscles relax and unwind and then just concentrate on your body breathing.

— Then when you are ready, take a gentle deep breath and then sigh the breath out — as if you are sighing any worry, tension or concern out of your body. As you sigh the breath out say the word 'relax' to yourself in your mind, smile and let all the muscles from your forehead to your feet go into floppy doll mode and unwind, relax and smooth out.

— Do the deep breathing routine three times.

— Then go back to breathing normally but continue with the word 'relax' as you breathe out, and continue to let those muscles relax and smooth out.

— Continue this for a few minutes and then use what we call 'guided imagery' or visualisation to help you really unwind. As you imagined the tape recorder and catastrophe scale in your head, this time imagine yourself in a very pleasant place, like a beach, garden, holiday scene. Lie back feeling very relaxed, very much in control. This is your time to take care of yourself. If you find the imagery difficult, just feel how relaxed and calming it would be. Do this for several more minutes.

— Just before you open your eyes and gently move into the rest of the day, run two or three short positive self-talks through your head. Things like 'I am a worthwhile person' and 'What do I want to achieve right now?'

— Slowly open your eyes, adjust to the light and gently move into the next activity in your day.

— If at all during the session you feel a little funny with your eyes closed, open your eyes for a short time, and then continue the technique when you are ready.

Longer relaxation techniques are also very good for us and can be very calming and useful. However, the compliance rate of people sticking to the longer techniques (generally 20 minutes) is very low. That's why I favour a shorter technique more often. Some of the useful longer techniques are things like deep muscle relaxation, autogenic training, transcendental meditation, self-hypnosis, yoga and tai chi. If you wish to pursue these, joining a group to do them may help you stick to them so you gain the benefits over a longer period of time.

GUIDED IMAGERY

I have already used several examples of how imagery can be very successfully used to remember certain techniques or to assist in the relaxation response. Let's expand that because the research shows that imagery is a powerful self-help technique, whether it is used for achieving in sport or in order to perform more effectively in areas of life in which we may have developed a phobia (exaggerated fear response). For our purpose we can use it to gain more control over worry by actually seeing ourselves in a manner that indicates *self-control, a positive manner, high self-esteem and a confident body language.*

The technique is to begin as for the quick relaxation technique.

Once we have completed the three deep breaths routine we again go back to breathing normally for a few minutes and then begin the *guided imagery.*

Imagine yourself standing in a field of lovely green short grass on a very gently sloping hill. You have a wonderful view of the countryside and a tree-lined river below.

See and sense yourself feeling fit, healthy, strong and confident as you are standing there with a warm gentle breeze on your face.

As you stand there feeling very much in control of yourself remind yourself that you have choices in life, you are free to be yourself and feel good about who you are. You are free to change anything about yourself you wish to.

If there are things about yourself you really do want to change, then imagine yourself feeling confident that you can do it. This may include seeing yourself worrying less and feeling more relaxed and capable, happy to be who you are.

Then imagine reaching out and drawing that person inside of you, so that over the next few weeks you will be working towards becoming more like that person.

Before you open your eyes remind yourself that you are important to look after and that you will work towards that positive image of yourself over the next few weeks.

Slowly open your eyes, get used to the light again, smile and get on with the rest of your day. The wise person knows that *you become what you think you are.* Set a positive image and believe in yourself. Then step by step move to where you wish to go. Pat yourself on the back for every step you take. Remember to build on what you *can* do, and what you *have* done.

SUMMARY

◆ Develop stickability.

◆ Use the catastrophe scale to help keep things in perspective.

◆ Thought stopping and thought switching will help to stop catastrophising thoughts.

◆ Troubleshoot yourself by shifting from automatic pilot to manual control from time to time.

◆ Focusing — looking at what we can do and what we have done, not at what we can't do and what we haven't done.

◆ Use the quick relaxation technique to relax and help keep things in perspective by unwinding.

◆ Guided imagery assists in building a positive self-image.

◆ Remember that the wise person knows *you become what you think you are*.

CHAPTER 8

Taking action

The techniques and ideas in the last few chapters are essential for a high quality life without unnecessary worries. Our thinking processes have a very powerful effect on our emotional state and on our behaviour and actions. Some of us will have acquired very positive, adaptive and solution-orientated attitudes and beliefs as we made our way through life, so it is a matter of making sure we look after them and troubleshoot them from time to time. Others of us will need to place more emphasis on the techniques mentioned and practise them regularly to gain the full benefit and to erase any bad habits.

However, if we put a lot of personal energy and focus into our attitudes and beliefs, and don't change our behaviour or actions we may tend to wear out, feel that the adaptive thinking does not work. This is very demotivating. This chapter looks at how we can back up our positive attitudes with positive and adaptive action.

How do we overcome worry through our actions? We have to overcome those minor or major fears and concerns through a process which is called, in psychological jargon, desensitisation. There will be more about this later.

AVOIDANCE
Avoiding things which we find unpleasant or which we feel we may have difficulty dealing with is a fairly common and under-

standable human response. We like
to stay within our 'comfort zone'
where we know what to expect, even
if the 'comfort zone' is fairly unac-
ceptable or lacking in the things we
consider important in life. While we
may understand why we often don't
take action to better our lot in life,
this does not mean it is the best
thing for us. So how do we move

ourselves from inaction to action and tackle those fears and
situations we worry about.

There may well be a whole range of very pleasant life events
out there waiting for us. At the moment we may have them in
the too hard basket.

THE BIG PICTURE — MANAGING LIFE

Everyone needs goals in life. If we don't have goals, we tend to
develop very maladaptive habits which will in turn tend to lock
us into those maladaptive comfort zones I have been talking
about.

So before we consider how to desensitise ourselves to fearful situations, we need to consider which situations are worth the effort. Of course, overcoming any fear can reduce worry and boost our self-esteem which helps us remain positively focused. However, if we overcome a meaningful and 'fearful' situation, or even if we achieve a goal we consider to be worthwhile, it can give us a real boost. The experience will prepare us to cope with more determination and less worry next time. So let's set some goals.

Consider the following list:

◆ psychological (emotional) well-being;

◆ health (physical) well-being;

◆ work (vocation);

◆ family;

◆ social (friends);

◆ leisure/recreational pursuits;

◆ spiritual issues;

◆ financial matters;

◆ self-growth/knowledge.

Now, rank them in order of their importance to you:
1 — most important to 9 — least important.

How satisfied do you feel in each of the life areas mentioned? That is, how well are you managing each, in terms of gaining satisfaction from that area of your life:
1 — not very satisfied to 10 — extremely satisfied.

Use the following checklist to gain a profile of yourself:

Importance	Life Area	How satisfied
_____	Psychological well-being	_____
_____	Health (physical)	_____
_____	Work (vocation)	_____

_____	Family	_____
_____	Social	_____
_____	Leisure/Recreation	_____
_____	Spiritual	_____
_____	Financial	_____
_____	Self-growth	_____

What does the profile tell you about yourself? Are there any indications where your worries may be coming from or why you are not managing those areas of your life well?

MAKING DECISIONS

An unbelievable amount of worry, frustration and self-doubt comes from procrastination — putting off decisions, not making our minds up, and not following through on things.

Now that we have considered those areas in life that are important and valued by us and how satisfied we are with them, let's stop any procrastination and select one area that we are going to work on and enhance for ourselves.

That area is _____
(Refer to the list of nine areas above.)

We now need to set a specific meaningful goal within that area, working out how to go about resolving the challenge and achieving your action plan to do just that. Before we jump in and begin to solve that challenge and achieve your goal, let's reflect on what a SMART goal is so you start off on the right foot:

◆ Specific — this addresses behaviour and results, not emotions. It narrows down what you want to do.

◆ Measurable — are you able to track and monitor your progress?

◆ Attributable — you need to be able to say 'I did that' and 'If it's to be, it's up to me'.

◆ Realistic — it should be something you can accomplish or set in motion in the next few weeks.

◆ Time framed — this is when you will achieve each step to your goal. Set deadlines.

PROBLEM-SOLVING/DECISION-MAKING

Let's work through the steps involved in making effective decisions for ourselves. Keep in mind that for some of you, this process may seem a little tedious. Once you have done it a few times you can then become a little less formal about the process. You will then tend to do it more automatically. If we don't take the time to learn how to do things properly, we often rush through them, leave out important processes, make poor decisions and then worry about the poor results we got!

Remember the old saying, 'an ounce of prevention is worth a pound of cure'.

So let's slow ourselves down and use the opportunity to fine tune our decision-making and problem-solving skills.

Step 1 — What is the goal/challenge I want to achieve?

Be specific, for example 'exercise three times a week'; don't be too general, like 'I want to be fit'.

Goal: _____

64

Step 2 — How do I feel about it? For example, uncertain, excited, confused, anxious, energised.

_____

Step 3 — Relax, unwind for a moment. Make sure you are not frowning, tense or frustrated. If so, use the quick relaxation technique to unwind.

Decision-making and problem-solving need to be fun, and a normal part of life. Learn to enjoy the challenge of embarking on new things and to relax while doing them.

Step 4 — Consider all possible solutions. Can you think of different ways of achieving your goal? List down the different things you could do, and different ways you could go about it.

_____

_____

_____

_____

_____

Step 5 — How might others go about achieving this goal?

_____

_____

_____

_____

Step 6 — List the things you could do in order of priority — 1 being your best idea, 2 your second best etc.

_____

_____

_____

_____

_____

Step 7 — Make a choice, select which option you will take. It may not be No. 1 or it may be another option high on your list. I am going to do:

_____

Step 8 — How will you do it? Form a plan of action. I need to:

Step 1._____

Step 2._____

Step 3._____

Step 4._____

Step 5._____

Step 6._____

Step 7._____

Step 8._____

Step 9 — When will you start? Set a date.

I will begin on:_____

I will review progress on:_____

Step 10 — Give yourself a pat on the back.

You deserve it. No 'gonna' excuses — you have formulated an action plan. Now get into it.

Can you think of any benefits to you of having the initial problem or challenge in your life? One I can think of is that it has led to you getting to this stage, understanding there is no need to worry or procrastinate about things. Just settle down and work out a solution as you have just done.

SUMMARY

◆ Follow attitude change with positive action.

◆ Beware of avoidance — it tends to lower self-esteem and self-confidence.

◆ Manage the big picture of your life.

◆ Set smart goals.

◆ Follow an effective problem-solving/decision-making process.

◆ How will you do it? Form an action plan.

CHAPTER 9

Overcoming fears, panic and anxiety

Quite often when we lay down a plan of action to resolve issues in our lives that have been a worry, and we see ourselves achieving those goals, we really begin to fire and nothing can hold us back. But what about those situations that we avoid because the very thought of doing something about them fills us with fear and panic? For some of us it would be a fear of heights, enclosed spaces, air travel, spiders or perhaps even just leaving home. Some situations are so minor or strange that we have no idea why we get so uptight, worried or panicky about them, yet we do, time after time, and we feel powerless and somewhat helpless about our situation. Don't panic, help is available and is generally very effective if you do the right things by following the right advice.

A procedure known as *systematic desensitisation* has proven to be extremely effective for overcoming fear-provoking situations, often referred to by psychologists as phobias or panic disorders.

There are different types of phobias:

Simple phobias — This is where we experience fear and anxiety when confronted by one particular thing such as spiders, heights or lifts. Sometimes the situations can seem rather bizarre, such as battery acid, small lizards, the dark, or even approaching traffic signals.

Social phobias — This is excessive fear and worry of being with other people and of being assessed by them. It is often associated with a concern that others are judging you. The most common social phobia is a fear of public speaking called *glossophobia*. Other common social phobias are meeting people, eating in front of others or signing your name in front of others. These phobias are very common, affecting one or two per cent of the population.

Shyness is not the same as having a social phobia. A shy person generally lacks some common social skills and is worried and anxious in most, if not all, social situations. Shyness is quite common, is generally not as severe in its effects and is not a clinical problem or a phobia.

Panic and agoraphobia — Panic and agoraphobia are closely related, and affect about five per cent of the population.

Panic is the sudden onset of intense fear and apprehension often associated with feelings of impending doom. The symptoms are rapid heart beat, shortness of breath or hyperventilation, sweating, shaking, depersonalisation (you are not really with yourself, you feel disorientated) and fears of dying, going mad or making a fool of yourself in public. People also become very sensitised to their symptoms and focus on them intensely. The attacks often seem to happen out of the blue, and it appears this is because they can be triggered by internal biological reactions, involving an increase in stress.

Agoraphobia is usually referred to as unreasonable fear and worry of leaving a safe place and going into open spaces. One of the major fears is being in a place or situation where you may have a panic attack and not be able to get help or get to 'safety'. We develop a 'what if?' syndrome — 'what if I have a panic attack, what if I embarrass myself, what if I have a heart attack?' People then worry that they may embarrass themselves or have a heart attack or the like. Psychologists sometimes call this phenomenon the *fear of fear*, and of course what happens is that we tend to avoid situations where this may happen or where we might not be able to get help or get to a place where we feel safe.

Even though we may feel we are the only ones experiencing these intense forms of worry, anxiety and physiological alarm responses, we are not. So don't feel stupid, weak or alone. You're among friends. However, you still need to do something about the disorder. These disorders normally start in early adult life.

When we avoid situations, we of course reinforce the fear, worry and uncertainty. We lower our self-confidence and feelings of control over the situation and remain feeling trapped and full of self-doubt.

WHAT TO DO

When worry, anxiety and our behaviour are seemingly so out of our control and we have developed a phobia, professional help from a registered and well qualified clinical psychologist may be the most appropriate course of action. If you feel that you can make it on your own, maybe with a friend as a supporter or buddy, then the following techniques will be of enormous benefit.

ATTITUDINAL CONTROL AND RELAXATION

The thought stopping and thought switching technique we have begun to practise, along with using the catastrophe scale are essential in getting our thinking straight to assess what is happening. To take the extreme worry and fear out of the situations we need to keep what is happening in perspective and shrink the worry.

Remind yourself that you are telling yourself this is awful, terrible, you can't stand it, but in terms of what could happen to us in *reality* (death, major accident etc.) this is really 10 out of 100 — not 90 as our reaction might suggest.

So work on using your self-talk, attitudes and belief system to keep things in perspective and to stop any distorted thinking running on for too long. Many of you with phobias may have already tried this, probably poorly, so give it another go. Armed with the techniques just mentioned, and also the quick relaxation technique we went through, we are ready for the next stage.

SYSTEMATIC DESENSITISATION

This refers to the process of gradually, and in a planned fashion, getting rid of the fear and worry about something, by approaching it step by step, learning to relax each step of the way. Instead of letting the fear and worry build up as we go into a situation we can get quite panicky or phobic about, we literally practise approaching that situation and going through it slowly and in a relaxed manner.

Step 1 — The beginning — levels of anxiety

Select that thing or situations which you are phobic about.

I would like to get rid of my fear of _____

Now break the situation into as many (up to 10) steps as you can. Each step needs to be added anxiety for you. Take, for example, a fear of flying. You decide to go somewhere and realise you need to fly. This might induce 10 per cent anxiety, worry and fear; buying or getting the tickets increases it to 20 per cent; packing to go to the airport — 30 per cent; driving to the airport — 40 per cent; through to the plane taking off with you on it — 80 per cent. The worst anxiety — 100 per cent might be turbulence in flight.

Now use the checklist below to do the same for your specific situation.

71

Situation	% of anxiety felt
	(low)
1._____	_____
2._____	_____
3._____	_____
4._____	_____
5._____	_____
6._____	_____
7._____	_____
8._____	_____
9._____	_____
10._____	_____
	(high)

This has been a great start. You have identified the hierarchy, that is, the things associated with increases in your fear and worry.

Step 2 — Imagery practice

We are ready to begin the process of desensitisation, or getting on top of that phobia. You need to know your previous checklist well, as that will be your guide. Here is a six week program to follow:

Day 1 — Once or twice on the first day, run through the following technique:

1. Get yourself in a comfortable situation on a chair, couch or bed and begin the quick relaxation technique you learned in Chapter 7. Run through this until after the three deep breaths when you are breathing normally again and continuing with the word 'relax' as you breathe out and so on.

2. Now the imagery practice. Keeping your eyes closed and continuing to relax yourself, imagine yourself doing step 1 of the checklist. As you see yourself doing it, keep yourself relaxed. Keep a smile on your face.

3. Once you have seen yourself in that scene for several minutes, stop the imagery. Continue to breathe in a normal fashion and once again say the word 'relax' to yourself as you breathe out, smile, and let all your body go into floppy doll routine. Do this relaxation technique for several minutes.

4. Now return to the imagery and keeping yourself relaxed, see yourself moving to step 2, feeling in control, smiling and continuing to let your whole body unwind and relax.

5. After a period of time (a few minutes) seeing yourself doing step 2, stop the imagery and go back to your breathing. Continue to breathe in a normal manner and once again say the word 'relax' to yourself as you breathe out, keep smiling and once again continue to let all your muscles unwind, smooth out and relax. Do this for a few minutes. If you find you are a little anxious after imagining yourself going through step 2, take a couple of deep breaths and sigh them out, immediately after the imagery, and then go back to breathing normally and follow the rest of this point as suggested.

6. You have nearly completed your first session. Before you open your eyes, get used to the light again, and then go about the rest of your day, say three or four short positive self-talks to yourself, like 'I will get on top of this', 'I am going to enjoy this challenge', 'I'm looking forward to the rest of the day'.

Then gradually open your eyes get used to the light again, smile and get into your next activity.

Well done. You have taken the first step to get control over something in your life that seemed out of control. Keep this going and you will have an excellent chance of being one of the 80 per cent of people who totally rid themselves of these fears and major worries.

Now to continue the *systematic desensitisation* process, proceed as you have begun and add one step to the imagery each day, so your practice calendar is as follows:

(One or two sessions per day imagining the same steps each session for that day)

Day 2 — Follow the same procedure as for Day 1, however now continue the procedure to step 3. After imagining each step use the relaxation procedure to ensure you return to or remain in a relaxed, controlled and pleasant state. If you want to or feel you need to, you can implement a relaxation procedure part way through each step.

Remember, the whole idea now is to replace the anxiety, fear and worry you experienced in these steps with a relaxation response. We are re-conditioning ourselves to a new pattern of responding.

Day 3 — As for Days 1 and 2, but continue your imagery through to step 4.

Day 4 — As for other days, but continue your imagery through to step 5.

Day 5 — Continue your imagery through to step 6.

Day 6 — Continue your imagery through to step 7.

Day 7 — Continue your imagery through to step 8.

Day 8 — As for other days, now continuing your imagery through to step 9.

Day 9 — At the end of Day 9, reward yourself a with meaningful pay off for your stickability!

Day 10 — Follow the same procedure as for Day 9.

You have completed your intensive course of imaginal desensitisation.

Now for the real thing. Out into the real world. What psychologists call *in vivo desensitisation*.

Continue with your imaginal desensitisation, at least several times a week to reinforce a feeling of control and of being relaxed and calm in those specific situations.

IN VIVO DESENSITISATION

This procedure now puts into practice what you have been doing in those sessions using imagery. Now, however, you actually *do* those steps in reality, relaxing yourself as you go through them. Once again you *gradually* move through the steps over a period of time. Set a program of gradually working through those steps over the next four to five weeks.

Your program might look something like this.

Week 1	Session 1 Tuesday Steps 1–2	Session 2 Thursday Steps 1–3
Week 2	Session 1 Monday Steps 1–3	Session 2 Friday Steps 1–4
Week 3	Session 1 Tuesday Steps 1–5	Session 2 Saturday Steps 1–7
Week 4	Session 1 Wednesday Step 1–8	Session 2 Saturday Steps 1–10
Week 5	Session 1 Tuesday Step 1–10	Session 2 Friday Steps 1–10

Write out a program and stick to it. Remember you are important to look after, so take some time to improve your quality of life.

Gradually work through Steps 1–10 over a five week period using the relaxation procedure as you go.

Once you have mastered one major fear or worry, move to another one if you have one, and work through the same process.

If you have difficulties and feel you have persevered, seek professional help from a clinical psychologist who is trained in cognitive behaviour therapy. This is not an admission of defeat, but rather a sign of personal strength that you will not be beaten or give up, so you move to the next level of support, advice and assistance.

SUMMARY

◆ Systematic desensitisation is a proven technique for overcoming your fears.

◆ There are different types of phobias and worries which vary in intensity.

◆ Develop a hierarchy of anxiety-producing situations.

◆ Imagery practice is a great starting point.

◆ In vivo (real life) practice is the finishing touch to overcoming the fear or phobia.

◆ With desensitisation we replace an anxiety response to a situation with a relaxed response.

CHAPTER 10

You know you're successful when . . .

Achieving a self-set goal in life can, and indeed ought, to be a great feeling. Success is a wonderful thing. It enhances our self-esteem, self-confidence and self-dignity. One of the major benefits is the feedback that yes, we can achieve many of the things that we want to in life.

Overcoming a worry habit is no different. We need to give ourselves a well-earned pat on the back for sticking at it and working through the issues and techniques involved.

So, how do we know if we have been successful in reducing our worrying and in implementing a far more rational, positive and solution-orientated approach to our daily living? The following pointers will give you a fairly accurate picture of just how successful you have been.

Use the pointers as a guide. If you have done well, keep whatever it is you are doing going. If you have not done so well, don't be discouraged. Reorganise yourself, and re-read Chapters 6–9. People vary in how quickly they get used to the techniques and how successful they are in implementing them. Remember the old saying 'practice makes perfect', so keep at it.

SUCCESS POINTERS

WELL-BEING

An overall sense of well-being is a good sign that we are on top of worry. Well-being is best defined as a feeling of physical and emotional health. So a bounce in your step, relaxed body and body language, a smile on your face, and a perception of your own good health are pretty sure indicators.

HUMOUR

A worry habit is a very effective way to destroy or dampen your sense of humour. Humour is a great stress reduction tool. It is also a fairly sure way of making and keeping friends. When our sense of humour starts to return we are beginning to get a handle on worry. A sign that we have worry well under control is when we can laugh at ourselves. This generally indicates that we are not worried about making mistakes or having to be perfect all the time — an impossibility for any human being.

SELF-ESTEEM

Do we like ourselves? Are we at ease with who we are? Can we accept ourselves, warts and all? Do we readily give ourselves a pat on the back for a job well done? Can we admit mistakes we make without becoming unduly defensive? Do we feel free to be who we are without excessive approval seeking or withdrawing from situations?

If you answered 'yes' or 'I do' to most of these questions or statements you have worry where it needs to be, well and truly under control.

RELATIONSHIPS

Our ability to feel at ease and relaxed around others can indicate low levels of worry, especially when accompanied by some of the other pointers. Are we understanding, accepting and patient with others? Do we take the time to listen and are we generally free of value judgments? Can we form close intimate relationships easily and do we maintain these over time? Do we speak and converse with people in a manner that encourages them to trust us and to speak their mind? Do others find that we are moody and unpredictable or even-tempered and generally very approachable?

POSITIVE HABITS

Positive habits are also a good indication of low levels of worry. Moderate to low levels of alcohol intake, a balanced, low fat diet, regular exercise, a good balance in life, reasonable work hours, limited cups of coffee per day and nil or very few cigarettes each day are positive habits we should develop. Do we make time for regular passive or active relaxation pursuits?

CHANGE

Can we keep a perspective on looking at the advantages of changing and the disadvantages of not changing, rather than seeing the disadvantages of changing and the advantages of not changing? Do we feel exhilarated and challenged by new things and new challenges, rather than overwhelmed and debilitated by them?

SELF-TALK

We're back to that tape recorder in our heads. Are we FARPSing regularly? Are we flexible, adaptable and able to incorporate new ideas? Is our self-talk generally positive and solution-orientated? Do we consider the positive things about people and what is happening in our world, or are those thoughts and beliefs still a bit negative, worrying and upsetting for us?

NOVELTY/COMFORT ZONE

Human beings seem to thrive on a certain amount of risk-taking.

SORTING OUT WORRY

If we don't feel at ease pursuing these types of events we can begin to 'rust out' or become under-stimulated, lethargic and, dare I say it, rather boring and bored. When this happens we can turn to negative addictions to cope. When we feel able to step outside our comfort zone and have a go we have worry parcelled up very neatly — enough to release a little adrenalin and get us ready for the new challenge.

Now lets see how you fare. You've had time to think about the issues, now complete the following checklist.

STAMPING OUT WORRY — A CHECKLIST

Response: Answer	Yes	No
I generally feel in good health	____	____
I find I smile a lot	____	____
I often laugh about things in life	____	____
If I make a silly mistake I often laugh about it	____	____
I give tasks in life my best shot	____	____
I know I am a worthwhile person	____	____
I like to get close to other people	____	____
I have enough close friends	____	____
I have no more than (men) 24 alcoholic drinks per week	____	____
(women) 12 alcoholic drinks per week	____	____
I am a normal weight to height ratio	____	____
New and different things generally excite me	____	____
With proper planning I can deal with anything	____	____
I generally think 'I can do it'	____	____
There are a lot of wonderful positive things happening in the world	____	____
I don't allow myself to stay bored for too long	____	____

It's challenging and exciting to push yourself that
extra step   ____ ____

I enjoy my own company   ____ ____

I am not unduly concerned about death   ____ ____

I believe life is here to be enjoyed   ____ ____

Score — your profile (add up the number of Yes answers):

15–20 Super effort — very well done. Your mission now is to maintain the attitudes and behaviours that you have in place. Keep them going, work on them, and troubleshoot them if you need to. You're a very worthy role model for others.

10–14 You're nearly there. With more practice you will break down even more of your worrying and be able to focus on more of the positives including solutions to problems. Make sure you practise — it is worth it.

5–9 You have just left the launch pad. There is still quite a distance to travel, but at least you're airborne. Keep firing those booster rockets. You know where you want to get to, so don't let anything divert you from your course. Practise, practise, practise.

0–4 Go back to Chapter 1 and read through this book again. I guarantee it really is easy to get the hang of the techniques I have described! If you have read it all once or twice, professional advice or counselling is the way to go — don't feel nervous about getting some advice — remember that you're important to look after. Chapter 13 will provide further assistance on how to get professional help.

It's important to have a high quality of life and maximise your potential. Worry will most definitely get in the way of you realising and becoming your best.

If you find you just can't get there with 'worry control' using your own resources, seek professional advice, assistance/or counselling.

SUMMARY

◆ Remember no great mountain was ever climbed, no marathon ever run, no book ever written, no sea ever crossed without someone taking those first steps.

◆ This book and the techniques described in it will not only help you take those first steps in combating worry, but take you a long way towards a good level of self-control.

CHAPTER 11

Living with a worrier

This can be an extremely frustrating situation for anybody, especially if you are fairly positive and solution-orientated in your attitudes and behaviours. Emotions can certainly run high here.

The effects of living with someone who worries a fair bit or a great deal, will be different for different people. Sometimes the effects will be minimal and really just a minor pain. However, in other instances the effects can have a major impact on someone's lifestyle, or quality of life. What are the range of responses and their effects on the worrier that we may have when in a personal or intimate relationship with the worrier?

SYMPATHY — POOR YOU

The response 'poor you, isn't it terrible', is often motivated by a feeling of duty that this is the way you should respond. We feel that we should (and we know how irrational shoulds are) also get upset and at least look as if we are terribly worried, or the person may feel we don't care.

Of course, this reaction may assist in exacerbating the worry, adding even more fuel to the fire, with the person really beginning to believe that he or she has a huge problem or there is a catastrophe pending. The person usually remains trapped in a 'poor me' trip. We will often get frustrated if the pattern of worry continues, and yet we are reinforcing it by just being sympathetic. Be careful with this approach.

PULL YOURSELF TOGETHER

This approach can be borne out of frustration, impatience or lack of understanding and empathy. We use words and phrases like 'wake up to yourself', 'you're not still going on about that' and 'forget it'. Our behaviour may indicate annoyance, anger and aggression.

What happens to the worrier when we react like this? They may feel belittled and allow their self-esteem to take a beating. They may go further into a 'poor me' trap. They may feel that you do not care for or about them at all, or that you feel they are weak and hopeless. Of course, they may get defensive and angry in return, and suddenly World War III has broken out.

OSTRICH RESPONSE

When we react with comments like: 'don't tell me, I don't want to know about it' or 'it's nothing to do with me', we avoid the situation and try to escape from it. Small bursts of this type of behaviour are okay, but if it goes on it can become maladaptive — the worrier gets no assistance, and we can develop a habit of avoiding things in life.

The effect on the worrier of this type of response is often a feeling of being alone with their worry and having no one to turn to. They think that perhaps they really are stupid, or that the situation is out of control. If the person is in need of lots of attention, they will of course just wander off and bother someone else. While you may think this is not a bad thing, at least they are leaving you alone, it really hasn't helped you or the worrier. Remember that they may return with more tales of woe and catastrophic happenings.

I'M OKAY APPROACH

This is a very interesting approach, where we use other people's worry habit to reinforce that we are okay. We say things like 'Oh I'm glad that didn't happen to me' or 'I don't know how you could stand it'. These comments are all designed not so much to show empathy for the person, but to make us feel better that we're doing okay.

Sometimes, the worrier may be totally unaware of what we have been doing, and in fact may feel we are sympathising with them. At other times this approach will just help to turn someone off and they will go and bother someone else or come back and bother you later. Every now and then someone will feel 'they thought it was a major thing, I guess I'm not coping too badly' or 'they thought it was terrible, how ever will I cope?'

SMART ALEC SYNDROME

This response is a real beauty. We come back at the person with things like 'what I would do is' or 'I'd show them, I'd say . . .' or 'that happened to me and I certainly did something about it'. It's the response that gives a message 'I'm an expert at this' or 'I'll use it as an opportunity to tell you about my life or my experiences — they're far more interesting than yours'.

Of course, for the worrier, this can be an immediate turn off. The person feels that they shouldn't have bothered, that the other person would not know the feeling. The worrier is then less likely to come to you for advice or to discuss issues with you in the future.

YOU THINK YOU'VE GOT PROBLEMS

This reaction overshadows the concerns of the other person, especially when we launch into a string of our own problems.

The worrier is immediately turned off, and feels and anger or sadness — 'they don't give a damn about me, so why bother?' The person is unlikely to discuss their worries or concerns with you in the future.

WHAT TO DO

If you are living with a worrier, or have any form of significant relationship with one there are things that you can do to minimise the effect on you and to assist that person in becoming more positive and optimistically focused in their approach to life. The most constructive approach you can take is to *be with* the person and then *do with* the person.

HOW TO BE WITH THE PERSON

What I mean by being with the person is to allow sufficient time and discussion on the point or points raised to understand, or at least try to understand, where the person is coming from. This means using good active listening skills:

◆ listening — paying attention, maintaining eye contact, remaining relaxed;

◆ clarifying — providing feedback to the person on what you think you have heard;

◆ levelling — being as honest as you can with the person about how you feel. This may help them get a more positive perspective on an issue.

When we use the skills just mentioned it is less likely that we will quickly go into one of the responses mentioned earlier that may not be all that constructive.

Once you feel you understand where the person is coming from and you have spent enough time being with the person move on to *doing with*.

HOW TO DO WITH THE PERSON

Doing with refers to moving on to an action plan. In being with the person, you gathered the facts; now it's time to work with them to find a solution to the worry and so stem its flow.

There is generally little point in getting into arguing the facts or almost appealing for a more positive view of the matter such as 'yes, but don't you think . . .' or 'wouldn't you agree that . . .'.

So the *doing with* phase focuses on helping the person to formulate an action plan which will help to alleviate the worry. This means assisting them in finding solutions or coming up with possible solutions yourself.

Once an action plan has been formulated, you may be able to act as a support for the person in getting started and completing the steps in the plan. The techniques described in Chapter 9 will be very useful here.

When someone who has been a chronic worrier begins to change the habit and take a few risks, or begins to focus on the positives, take every opportunity to reinforce and encourage those attitudes and behaviours.

WHEN ENOUGH IS ENOUGH

At times when all else has been tried, there may come a point when enough is enough. We need to decide when that is. If our own quality of life is being constantly eroded by a worrier, we may have to remove ourselves from that situation. It is our responsibility to take ownership of our own destinies, including surrounding ourselves with positive thinking people and keeping a reasonable balance of activities in our lives. If we do not do this we may end up a victim in the whole affair, even when we initially started off as a helper.

An indication that we really do need to be careful is when we decide to *give up* and join the worrier, or give in because the hassles are just not worth it. We may then stop doing things we enjoy, or stop planning things because they never eventuate or become too difficult when we try to involve the worrier.

Encouraging the person to seek professional help is always a very useful and recommended option. Some people can be prompted to seek help to assist you in coping — this is a useful approach if the person is reluctant to seek counselling on their own behalf. Another option is to seek advice and counselling for yourself if you feel rather helpless about changing the situation.

Marriage or relationship counselling may also be a good idea to assist both people in coping better and to prompt an honest reflection on problems.

CHECKLIST — ACTION PLAN

Do I live with a worrier? (yes/no) _____

How do I know he or she is a worrier? _____

How does it affect me? _____

How have I been dealing with it? _____

What do I need to do? _____

How will I know I've been successful? _____

SUMMARY

◆ The effects of living with a worrier vary greatly.

◆ The range of responses to the worrier include:
   sympathy;
   pull yourself together;
   ostrich response;
   I'm okay response;
   smart alec syndrome;
   you think you've got problems.

◆ What to do? *Be with* the person. Gain an understanding of how they feel. Then *do with* the person. Help them formulate an action plan.

◆ Be careful of becoming a victim.

◆ Check the checklist.

◆ Professional help may be necessary.

CHAPTER 12

Memory joggers

This chapter serves as a memory jogger for the important aspects and issues that have been discussed in the previous chapters, and that I feel are worthy of quickly revisiting to make sure we have our ideas and techniques in order.

The idea is to see how many of the questions posed you can come up with answers for. You then check your answers, chapter by chapter. Pencil in those answers which you had difficulty with, or actually had wrong or incomplete answers for. Enjoy the challenge.

1. A brief definition — what is worry?

_____

_____

_____

2. Can worry be useful? How?

_____

_____

_____

3. Name four common things we worry about. Tick two which apply to you.

_____

_____

_____

_____

4. Do you worry too much? What worrying attitudes/thoughts are you aware that you have?

_____

_____

_____

5. What are the effects of worry on you?

Physical	Physiological	Psychological
_____	_____	_____
_____	_____	_____
_____	_____	_____

Emotional	Interpersonal (interacting with others)
_____	_____
_____	_____
_____	_____

6. So, briefly, why do we worry?

_____

_____

_____

7. What can we call the thing in your head that stores your memories in it?

_____

8. Name three techniques which help to get control over worry, anxiety and fear.

1._____

2._____

3._____

9. What are the steps in problem-solving/decision-making?

_____

_____

_____

_____

_____

10. How would you describe 'systematic desensitisation'?

_____

_____

_____

_____

_____

_____

11. Name four success pointers that indicate you are coping well with worry.

_____

_____

_____

_____

PERSONAL ACTION PLAN

1. What particular worries do you need to work on?

_____

_____

_____

_____

2. What are you doing, or going to do, about one particular worry or worry habit?

Step 1._____

Step 2._____

Step 3._____

Step 4._____

Step 5._____

Step 6._____

3. How will you know when you are successful?

_____

_____

_____

_____

4. The major benefits for you in resolving this/these issues are:

_____

_____

_____

_____

5. As I achieve more self-control over this/these issues I will reward myself by:

_____

_____

_____

_____

Well done. It's important to take the time to help yourself. At the end of the day, it's all about stickability, so keep at it.

CHAPTER 13

Sources of assistance

WHY SEEK PROFESSIONAL HELP?

If you feel you need more guidance or extra assistance in dealing with your worrying, anxiety or fear, then do it. Professional advice or counselling is for people who decide they are going to take control over their lives, and so it is a very real sign of personal strength. It is not a sign of being weak or out of control.

So, following the reading of this book and exposure to the type of techniques necessary to break the worry habit, if you feel you still need some extra assistance, then do it. All that remains then is to ensure you obtain the right advice, support or counselling. This means you need to know what types of counsellors to see and how to find them.

CHOOSING ASSISTANCE — WHO DO I NEED TO SEE ?

Make sure the psychologist you choose is registered in your State. Clinical psychologists who are trained in what are termed the cognitive-behavioural forms of counselling and therapy, especially rational emotive therapy, are the professionals you need to see. These psychologists are generally in private practice or work for Community Health Services or large hospitals.

This particular style of advice, counselling and therapy is aimed at making sure we learn how to think and develop attitudes that are rational. As we have learned, this will then have a very positive impact on our behavioural and emotional state.

HOW DO I FIND THEM?

Psychologists are located under P in the Yellow Pages. These are generally psychologists in private practice, so you will pay for their services. Fees vary as widely as from $60–$140 per session. The fee recommended by the Australian Psychological Society per hour session was around $140 at the time this book was written. To check, you can always call the society on Freecall 1800 333 497. Remember, you sometimes really do get what you pay for.

Community Health Centres, Mental Health Teams and your local large hospital may also have psychologists on staff who provide services to the general community. These services are generally free. Some hospitals do have specialist anxiety disorder clinics.

Relaxation, assertiveness and stress management groups conducted at Community Health Centres and elsewhere can also provide valuable skills.

If you find yourself in a desperate situation, overwhelmed by worry late at night, services such as Lifeline can be excellent in an emergency, and you will find a list of the Community Services in the beginning of the white pages of the phone book.

Your local general practitioner will also be able to refer you to a well regarded psychologist.

BEWARE!

MEDICATION

Prescribed medications may help in the short-term if you are overcome by sudden unexpected major happenings in your life. If taken for long periods of time, you can develop both a physiological and psychological dependency on them. The effects of these dependencies are often worse than the original worry problem, so be cautious. If a medical practitioner or psychiatrist has you on medication for 'worry' make sure you discuss this with them regularly, and get a referral to someone who can guide you in learning self-help techniques — generally a trained cognitive behavioural psychologist. If in doubt get a second opinion — this is your right.

LONG-TERM PSYCHOANALYSIS

Generally speaking, this is a waste of time, energy and money. There are far better techniques for assisting people with 'worry' problems, to which the research testifies quite clearly. Beware of the 'three times a week for five years' types. It is definitely my advice is to get a second opinion if you find yourself in that situation.

FRINGE DWELLERS

These are so-called 'counsellors', who deal in para-psychological techniques such as re-birthing, or repressed memory syndrome. This can again be a real waste of time and money if you are serious about taking control of your own life. As with long-term psychoanalysis, these techniques can foster dependency, drain your money, and in some instances set you up to get involved with unusual groups. These techniques can be delivered by groups who prey on the emotionally vulnerable, so be careful to check things out thoroughly.

Remember that you are important to look after. If you really need professional assistance, don't be afraid to get it.

So all the very best for your future journey through life. Be positive, seek solutions, beat the worry habit and enhance your quality of life — you deserve it!

FURTHER READING

Brecht, G. *Sorting out Self-esteem*, Prentice Hall, Sydney, 1996.

Brecht, G. *Sorting out Stress*, Prentice Hall, Sydney, 1996.

Brecht, G. *Sorting out Goals*, Prentice Hall, Sydney, 1996.

Burns, D. *The Feeling Good Handbook*, William Morrow, New York, 1989.

Ellis, A. *How to stubbornly refuse to make yourself miserable about anything, yes, anything!* Pan Macmillan, Sydney, 1991.

Montgomery, R. *The Truth about Success and Motivation*, Lothian, Melbourne, 1987.

Seligman, M. *What You Can Change and What You Can't: The Complete Guide to Successful Self-improvement*, Random House, Sydney 1994.

Tanner, S. and Ball, J. *Beating the Blues: A Self-Help Approach to Overcoming Depression*, Doubleday, Sydney, 1991.

INDEX